D1065286

{ Little-Known
FACTS
ABOUT
Well-Known
PLACES }

NEW ORLEANS

# { Little-Known FACTS ABOUT Well-Known PLACES }

# NEW ORLEANS

## VICTOR DORFF

ST. JOHN THE BAPTIST PARISH LIBRARY
2920 NEW HIGHWAY 51
LAPLACE, LOUISIANA 70068

## FALL RIVER PRESS

New York

## FALL RIVER PRESS

New York

An Imprint of Sterling Publishing
387 Park Avenue South
New York, NY 10016

FALL RIVER PRESS and the distinctive Fall River Press logo
are registered trademarks of Barnes & Noble, Inc.

© 2012 by Sterling Publishing Co., Inc.

This 2012 edition published by Fall River Press.

All rights reserved. No part of this publication may be reproduced,
stored in a retrieval system, or transmitted, in any form or by any means,
electronic, mechanical, photocopying, recording, or otherwise,
without prior written permission from the publisher.

ISBN 978-1-4351-0432-7

Distributed in Canada by Sterling Publishing
*c/o* Canadian Manda Group, 165 Dufferin Street
Toronto, Ontario, Canada M6K 3H6
Distributed in the United Kingdom by GMC Distribution Services
Castle Place, 166 High Street, Lewes, East Sussex, England BN7 1XU
Distributed in Australia by Capricorn Link (Australia) Pty. Ltd.
P.O. Box 704, Windsor, NSW 2756, Australia

For information about custom editions, special sales, and premium and
corporate purchases, please contact Sterling Special Sales at 800-805-5489
or specialsales@sterlingpublishing.com.

Manufactured in China

2 4 6 8 10 9 7 5 3 1

www.sterlingpublishing.com

# INTRODUCTION

Music, food, and natural disasters are quintessentially New Orleans. But if all you can think of when someone says "Big Easy" are jazz, *Mardi Gras*, and Hurricane Katrina, you're in for a treat.

This city has a rich and strange history. In its first century, New Orleans was passed from one country to another like a hot potato, sometimes without anyone telling the residents that their nationality had changed.

Most of the architecture in the *French* Quarter is in the *Spanish Colonial* style.

New Orleans is the birthplace of the American casino, the cocktail, and

dental floss. It's where pirates joined with American heroes to fight the British, and the commander in chief of the U.S. military forces turned out to be a spy for Spain.

Then, there's the New Orleans pine tree that's been to the moon.

This has always been a city of passion—with more duels fought here than in any other American city—and a city of equal opportunity, where women during the Civil War formed a formidable resistance movement against the U.S. occupation. Even people of color were free to own slaves.

Heard about the mummies who went to the Super Bowl? Keep reading!

Look for these other
titles in the series:

Little-Known
FACTS
ABOUT
Well-Known
PLACES

DISNEYLAND ✦ IRELAND
ITALY ✦ NEW YORK
PARIS ✦ TEXAS
WALT DISNEY WORLD

Long before there was Las Vegas, there was New Orleans.

The first gambling casinos in America opened in New Orleans in 1822, mostly on the waterfront, and were frequented by rough-and-tumble men of the river.

John Davis, a wealthy arts patron, introduced the concept of a 24-hour, all-you-can-eat, luxury casino in 1827. He put up a string of buildings along Orleans Street to accommodate the clientele who came to visit the "Temples of Chance."

By 1835, pressure from the anti-gambling movement forced New Orleans to end licensed gambling. Davis went back to being a major supporter of opera.

**P**oker and craps entered North America by way of New Orleans.

In the early 1800s, French settlers played a card game called *Poque* (po-KAY), which involved betting and bluffing.

Craps is another descendent of a French game. Bernard de Marigny brought a game called Hazard to New Orleans, where it caught on among slaves and the French Creoles, who called it *Crapaud* (the French word for "toad").

Professional gamblers spread the games through the rest of the country via the riverboats, as did slaves who were sent to live throughout the South.

*aubourg Marigny*, the New Orleans neighborhood downtown of the French Quarter, was created when Bernard De Marigny subdivided his plantation in 1805 (reportedly to help pay his gambling debts) and began selling parcels to the free people of color.

Frenchmen Street—lined with restaurants, nightclubs, and coffeehouses—has become the hot spot for live music and entertainment in this up-and-coming district.

ew Orleans' original French name, *La Nouvelle Orléans*, was given in honor of Philippe II, Duc d'Orleans, the regent of France under King Louis XV. (The British did the same with New York, which was named after James, Duke of York).

✓ New Orleans has several nicknames, including "The City That Care Forgot" and "The Crescent City." The former refers to the mood of this carefree city and its fun-loving population. The latter reflects the fact that the Mississippi River runs around the city in a crescent shape.

Using one particular nickname for New Orleans—"The Big Easy"—could get a visitor into a little trouble. Some natives take offense at hearing their city referred to that way, just as San Franciscans tend to hate the moniker "Frisco."

No one is quite sure of the origin of The Big Easy sobriquet. Musicians of the early 1900s may have invented it, or it may have been the name of a dance hall or a dance.

That might explain why, despite the residents' objections to the phrase, the local music industry awards are handed out by The Big Easy Foundation and called The Big Easy Music Awards.

New Orleans may very well have been the birthplace of "Dixie" itself!

The Citizens' Bank of Louisiana, operating in the French Quarter since the 1830s, issued its own $10 note, which it marked in both English ("ten") and French ("*dix*").

One theory posits that people referred to New Orleans as the "land of the *dix*," which eventually became "Dixieland" and was applied more generally to the entire South.

In the early 18th century, French settlers lived along the Atlantic coast, from Virginia to Nova Scotia. France referred to that area as Acadia and the residents as Acadians.

By 1760, the British had forced most Acadians out of the territory, either back to France or to another part of the North American continent.

Many eventually found their way to New Orleans, with its familiar language and customs.

On arrival, the name "Acadians" morphed into "Cajuns," which refers to the descendents of those exiled people.

Both the French and Spanish drew a distinction between settlers who were born in Europe and European descendents who were born in the New World, regardless of ethnic background.

Natives of the New World with European ancestry—whether pure or mixed with African or Native American heritage—were referred to as "Creoles."

French and Spanish colonists viewed race differently than their British counterparts. From the beginning, New Orleans was home to people of color who were born free, slaves who had been freed or purchased their freedom, and Haitians who had won their freedom in battle.

Thus, New Orleans society evolved into a unique three-tiered structure: the white ruling class, slaves, and free people of color.

Free people of color were allowed to be educated, to own property, and to succeed in the arts and business. They also were allowed to own slaves, and some of them did.

Free people of color (and their descendents) became known as Louisiana Creoles.

Whites and free people of color were legally forbidden to marry, but that didn't stop liaisons, whether based on love or convenience.

In the North, such relationships were a source of shame and kept hidden from view.

Not so in New Orleans. On the contrary, these relationships were very much a part of life, with their own set of rules.

*Plaçage* (from the French *placer*, or to place) was the socially accepted process of creating formal, if not legally recognized, relationships between a white man and a free woman of color.

A white man might provide a *placée* (placed woman) with a home in a Creole neighborhood—and even live there with her for a time.

Among the Creoles, a *plaçage* was recognized as a *mariage de la main gauche* ("left-handed marriage"). A *placée* would take the man's name, as would any children they had together. He was expected to care for them as he would in any family relationship.

White society did not recognize *plaçage* as a legitimate union, so white men also were free to formally marry. Thus, in addition to having a *plaçage* and family in New Orleans, a white man might have a white marriage and family on a plantation out of town.

In many cases, upon a man's death, his *placée* and their children could legally inherit his property.

The Roman Catholic heritage of the French and Spanish colonial rule still heavily influences New Orleans.

Carnival, *Mardi Gras*, and the Day of the Dead all have roots in Christianity, but the traditions and celebrations have taken on a secular importance unique to this city.

The Feast of the Epiphany, on the twelfth night after Christmas when the three wise men were said to have brought gifts to the newborn Jesus, marks the beginning of Carnival.

Ash Wednesday is the beginning of Lent, when many Christians begin a forty-day period of sacrifice prior to Easter. The day before Ash Wednesday, unofficially set aside for a final day of indulgence prior to self-deprivation, is *Mardi Gras* (literally, "Fat Tuesday").

he King Cake party marks the beginning of Carnival in New Orleans.

A King Cake, decorated in purple, green, and gold, is served as part of the celebration of the Feast of the Epiphany.

Hidden inside the cake, a small figure of a baby—usually, but not always, plastic—represents Jesus. The person whose slice of cake contains the baby is expected to throw the holiday party the following year.

Hundreds of thousands of King Cakes are baked, sold, and eaten in New Orleans to mark the start of the season, and a variety of New Orleans King Cakes now are shipped worldwide via Internet orders.

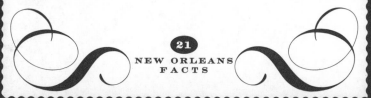

**P**urple, green, and gold supposedly were chosen as the official colors of *Mardi Gras* by Grand Duke Alexis Alexandrovich Romanoff during his visit to New Orleans in 1872, but other explanations abound:

They are the colors of the Catholic Church Year.

They are the colors of myrrh, frankincense, and gold, respectively.

They just look good together.

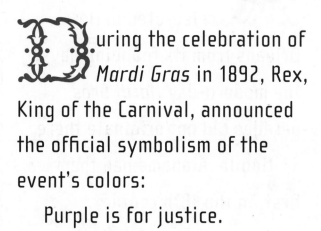

During the celebration of *Mardi Gras* in 1892, Rex, King of the Carnival, announced the official symbolism of the event's colors:

Purple is for justice.

Green is for faith.

Gold is for power.

Although the holiday was celebrated in New Orleans from its founding days, the modern-day *Mardi Gras* parades did not originate there.

Mobile, Alabama had them first, in the 18th century.

People from Mobile gathered in New Orleans in the middle of the 19th to bring their traditions to the Crescent City.

In the early years of *Mardi Gras* in New Orleans, celebrations were informal and sporadic events. By the middle of the 19th century, some feared the tradition was dying out.

To rejuvenate *Mardi Gras* celebrations in New Orleans, six Anglo-Americans met in December 1856 and formed the Mystick *Krewe* of Comus. They planned a torch-lit, nighttime parade of marching bands and rolling floats, which sparked the traditions we know today.

The Rex Organization was formed in 1872 to reinvigorate the celebration of *Mardi Gras* and the city of New Orleans, which was still recovering from the Civil War.

The birth of Rex, which officially was incorporated as the School of Design, was prompted by the scheduled visit of Russia's Grand Duke for the holiday.

A king called Rex, chosen from among the Rex Organization members, led the first daytime *Mardi Gras* parade, riding a horse through the streets of revelers, who naturally fell in line to follow along.

From there, the traditions just grew.

In the years following its initial success in 1872, Rex issued a proclamation in the name of the King of Carnival inviting all his "subjects" to come to the imaginary kingdom's Capital City for a celebration of *Mardi Gras*.

These proclamations somehow made their way to railroad stations around the country, and people from far and wide flocked to New Orleans for the party.

**T**oday, Rex, King of Carnival, arrives in New Orleans by boat on the Monday before *Mardi Gras*. Government leaders join the festivities by greeting the King and surrendering the keys to the city to him.

On *Mardi Gras*, the King presides over an elaborate parade, then appears at the premier Carnival Ball, which is the culmination of the celebrations.

Rex threw the first trinkets from floats to onlookers in the 1870s. They were inexpensive, glass-bead necklaces imported from Czechoslovakia.

Later, Rex introduced the doubloon, a medallion stamped for the occasion, as another "throw" item.

In modern years "throws" also have included cups, Frisbees, and coconuts.

However, coconuts—a much coveted "throw"—are no longer thrown. In 1988, the city decided they were too dangerous. Today, the hand-painted coconuts are gently given to the crowd by members of the *Krewe* of Zulu, who introduced the coconut throw to *Mardi Gras* in 1910.

Individual *krewe* members spend hundreds of dollars each of their own money for the trinkets they throw from the floats to the revelers in the streets.

The Mystick *Krewe* of Comus provided the final parade of the night for more than one hundred *Mardi Gras* celebrations.

In 1991 the city of New Orleans decided that applicants for parade licenses could not discriminate and required that membership rosters be submitted with the application. Comus, a private and exclusive club, had incorporated secrecy as one of its fundamental tenets. Therefore, the group chose to cancel its parade rather than change its policy.

There have been no Comus parades since then. (But that doesn't mean *Mardi Gras* is without parades...)

Since the formation of the Mystick *Krewe* of Comus, many other *krewes* have formed with the sole purpose of producing a *Mardi Gras* parade.

As more *krewes* come along, the timing and locations of parades have grown to accommodate them.

Today, New Orleans has a parade every night for weeks before *Mardi Gras*, and parades appear in more and more neighborhoods.

Parades in the French Quarter, however, ended in 1972 because the narrow streets were ill equipped to handle the increasingly larger floats.

ecause parades no longer pass through the French Quarter, the neighborhood isn't officially part of today's *Mardi Gras* festivities.

However, the French Quarter's Bourbon Street is home to several strip clubs, and police enforcement of morality there is somewhat looser than in the rest of the city. As a result, exhibitionists on Bourbon Street are willing to trade a glimpse of flesh for souvenir trinkets. Because nudity tends to attract a disproportionate amount of media attention, some people have the impression that *Mardi Gras* is all about college students who "flash for beads."

In fact, however, that falls under a different category of entertainment.

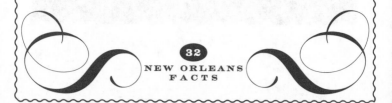

In the 1953 movie *Abbott and Costello Go to Mars*, the comedians play two hapless characters who inadvertently launch themselves in a rocket that was supposed to go to the red planet.

Instead, the rocket lands in New Orleans during *Mardi Gras*, but the men can't tell the difference.

In 1875 Louisiana declared *Mardi Gras* an official state holiday.

Today, it is said that the population of New Orleans doubles with tourists during *Mardi Gras*.

The 2009 *Mardi Gras* celebration generated an estimated $322 million in revenue for the city, according to a study commissioned by the Carnival *Krewe* Civic Fund.

That amount is more than 1 percent of the revenue generated by the city annually. Thus, the return on the city's investment in *Mardi Gras* is an estimated $4.48 for every dollar spent.

*Mardi Gras krewes* began as secret societies with invitation-only memberships. Blacks from the inner city generally were not included. Instead, they developed their own *krewes*, naming themselves after Native American tribes.

These original *Mardi Gras* Indians sometimes used the parades as an opportunity to settle scores between rival gangs, hiding behind masks, costumes, and the general chaos of the day.

In 1987, the New Orleans *Mardi Gras* Indian Council was formed to promote more peaceful celebrations. In 1992, the Big Chiefs of the major "tribes" gathered in a show of unity.

Today, that hostility has been replaced with a theatrical display of folk art, music, and dance.

*Mardi Gras* Indians spend as much as a year designing and creating the masks and costumes they wear on parade.

The leader of a tribe—usually the oldest member or the one with the greatest sewing ability or singing voice—is called the Big Chief.

Other "officials" of the tribe include a Spy Boy (who scouts during parades to find rival gangs), a Flag Boy (responsible for carrying the tribal flag), and a Wild Man (who clears a path for the Big Chief).

New Orleans has as many as 50 different tribes, each of which picks its own time and route for a parade.

When tribes meet while on parade, the confrontations are seemingly fierce, but the contest is over which Big Chief is the "prettiest" and which tribe has the most singing and dancing talent.

Tribes march during *Mardi Gras*, of course, but they also march on St. Joseph's Day (March 19th, the holiday honoring the spouse of the Virgin Mary) and on "Super Sunday," the Sunday closest to St. Joseph's Day.

New Orleans has a general law against wearing a mask to hide one's identity.

That law is suspended on *Mardi Gras*, enabling people in the street to wear masks for only that day.

On the other hand, revelers on *Mardi Gras* floats are *required* by law to wear masks.

*Mardi Gras* is an organic event—one that springs to life without anyone specific in charge.

Although *Mardi Gras* has generated a lot of revenue for New Orleans by encouraging tourism, the lack of central authority prevented anyone from being designated as an official sponsor of the event for the first hundred years or so.

Hurricane Katrina changed that.

In 2006, city officials were concerned that dwindling public coffers would prevent New Orleans from successfully controlling the crowd and cleaning up afterward.

As a result, the city turned to corporate America, and the Glad Products Company became the first official sponsor of *Mardi Gras*.

It may seem wrong to make an academic and archival study of something as spontaneous and carefree as *Mardi Gras*, but the carnival spirit plays too big a role in shaping the culture of New Orleans not to have its own year-round venue.

Sure enough, *Mardi Gras: It's Carnival Time* is a permanent exhibit at the Louisiana State Museum. Using interactive displays, costumes, and artifacts, the exhibit provides a way to enjoy the spirit of the festival no matter what time of year a visitor arrives in New Orleans.

All Souls Day on November 1st is a Roman Catholic holiday of prayer and remembrance of souls in purgatory, waiting to go to heaven.

All Saints Day is called the Day of the Dead in New Orleans, and Catholics and non-Catholics celebrate. Cemeteries are filled with people who come to paint the tombs, care for the graves, and remember the lives of their loved ones.

People often bring a picnic lunch and spend the day at the cemetery, creating a social atmosphere.

The holiday celebrates lives well lived, rather than mourning for people who are gone. Its observance crosses religious, social, and economic lines to include everyone.

When the French began to build New Orleans in 1721, it was a rectangular area of streets laid out in a grid. The *Place d'Armes* (now called Jackson Square) was the town square and was close to the Mississippi River (or "on the inside of town").

That entire rectangular area forms the heart of today's New Orleans, and it is called the *Vieux Carré* (Old Square) or the French Quarter.

Over the years, as the city expanded, it followed the curves of the Mississippi River, which is how it got the "Crescent City" nickname.

New Orleans has its own internal compass when it comes to directions.

Forget North, South, East, West. Get used to Uptown, Downtown, In, and Out.

Up and Down refer to the direction of the Mississippi. That is, downtown is the direction of the river flow (down river).

The winding river passes below New Orleans and then flows generally northward as it curves back up along the east side. So, loosely speaking, downtown is northbound, and uptown refers to southbound travel.

"In" refers to the direction toward the river, and Out is away, toward Lake Pontchartrain.

The original plans for New Orleans in 1721 called for a church to be built across the street outside the town square.

The first St. Louis Church was built in 1727, but that church was destroyed in a fire in 1788. In 1794, when the church was rebuilt, it was designated as a cathedral and opened on Christmas Eve.

Today, St. Louis Cathedral is the oldest continuously active cathedral in the United States.

St. Louis Cathedral is flanked on either side by the Cabildo (house of the colonial government) and the Presbytere (erected on the site of a former monastery for Capuchin monks). Both were built in the 1790s, although the second floor of the Presbytere wasn't finished until 1813.

The Cabildo, after its time as town hall, served as the Louisiana State Supreme Court. Today, it is the main building of the Louisiana State Museum.

The Presbytere began as a commercial building, became a courthouse in 1834, and has been part of the Louisiana State Museum since 1911.

**B**oth the Cabildo and the Presbytere added third floors during renovations in the 1840s, and both were topped with matching cupolas.

In 1915, a Category 4 hurricane destroyed the Presbytere cupola. Repairs were made to the roof, but the cupola was not replaced at the time.

When Hurricane Georges damaged the building again in 1998, architects decided to restore the building by adding a cupola.

The job wasn't finished until 2005, but today, the Cabildo and Presbytere are a matched set once again.

In the 1850s, the city renamed the *Place d'Armes* as Jackson Square to honor Andrew Jackson, who saved the city from the British in the War of 1812. At the time, however, the French Quarter had fallen into disrepair, and there was talk of tearing it down and replacing it with something more modern.

The Baroness Michaela Pontalba, one of the richest women in New Orleans at the time, recognized the historic nature of the French Quarter and developed a plan to revive it.

She designed two apartment buildings on the square: the Pontalba Apartments, which took two and a half years to build and cost $302,000.

Today, the city and state each owns one, and there is a waiting list to become a resident.

NEW ORLEANS
FACTS

The 1850 House in the Lower Pontalba Building offers a glimpse of life in another time.

The historic home is refurbished to show tourists how a middle-class family lived when the Baroness Pontalba opened her famed apartment buildings.

In 1897, New Orleans Alderman Sidney Story found the solution to the blight of prostitution that was plaguing his city: Confine it to a single district to isolate it from the neighborhoods whose falling property values were causing concern among honorable citizens.

For the next 19 years, the zone created by the alderman's legislation was the only government-sanctioned red-light district in the country, which ironically came to be known as Storyville.

With profits estimated as high as a million dollars per month, Storyville generated income for some rather respectable landlords, such as Tulane University and the Archdiocese of New Orleans.

The era ended in 1917 when the U.S. Navy decided prostitution had no place near naval bases.

The 1978 movie *Pretty Baby*, featuring Brooke Shields as a 12-year-old prostitute, is set in Storyville during its final days as a legal red-light district.

Jazz, the quintessentially American music, was emerging from New Orleans at about the same time as Storyville was enjoying its heyday.

Most of the "sporting houses" (bordellos) employed a solo piano player, usually referred to as the "Professor."

"Jelly Roll" Morton was one such "Professor."

Buddy Bolden and his band also grew out of Storyville.

Louis Armstrong was born there.

Louis Armstrong was not yet a teenager when he was arrested for firing a gun in the street as part of a New Year's celebration in 1913.

Sent to live in the New Orleans Colored Waifs' Home for Boys, Armstrong studied music—singing, percussion, and the trumpet.

When he left the home at age 14, Armstrong worked during the day and spent his nights listening to jazz musicians playing the streets of Storyville.

Joe "King" Oliver became Armstrong's mentor, helping launch the career of one of the most influential American musicians of the 20th century.

**P**erhaps this doesn't need to be mentioned, but...

Storyville was the red-light district in New Orleans at the turn of the 20th century.

Storyland is the name of a children's playground with slides and rides in New Orleans' City Park.

They are not to be confused.

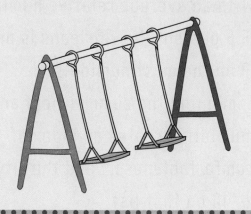

New Orleans has many great qualities, but the weather isn't one of them. The city ranks in the top 10 of three lists you won't see in any of the tourist brochures: wettest, most humid, and most uncomfortable cities in the United States.

It's No. 8 on the wettest list, with 50-plus inches per year.

With an average relative humidity of 75.5 percent, New Orleans is only No. 9 on the most humid list.

Combining the summer heat and the humidity creates an index of "uncomfortableness," and the city is No. 10 on that list.

Not every city in America can boast a pine tree that has been to the moon, but New Orleans can.

Astronaut Stuart Roosa was the command module pilot on Apollo 14 in 1971, and he brought some seeds with him on his trip to the moon.

New Orleans was given one of those germinated seeds in 1983, and it is now growing along the city's Riverwalk.

After surveying the land around New Orleans and finding no place that was not flooded in springtime, French explorer Jean-Baptiste Le Moyne de Bienville wrote home in 1708, "I do not see how settlers can be placed on this river."

Nevertheless, the strategic nature of the region at the mouth of the Mississippi River was too important to leave unprotected, so the French established a colony at New Orleans about 10 years later.

For nearly 300 years, nature has made it difficult for New Orleans to survive, and New Orleans seems to like it that way.

Militarily and economically, New Orleans is in a strategically important position. Thomas Jefferson observed that whoever possessed New Orleans would be the natural enemy of the United States, because the city is at the mouth of the river that supplies the Midwest.

Geographically, however, the location leaves a lot to be desired. As early as 1722, barely one year after construction had begun on what is now the French Quarter, a hurricane hit New Orleans and nearly wiped everything out.

Ever since, engineers and Mother Nature have been taking turns building defenses against flooding and knocking them down again.

From 1817 to 1905, more than 41,000 people in New Orleans died of yellow fever.

The last epidemic in the city was in 1905 because by then officials realized that the infection was spread by mosquitoes.

The worst epidemic was in 1853, when nearly 8,000 people—almost 7 percent of the city's population— lost their lives to the disease.

Since 1759, an average of two hurricanes have hit the Louisiana coast every three years, flooding New Orleans 38 times. That's not counting flooding simply as a result of over-abundant rainfall.

In between, there have been catastrophic fires and crippling epidemics.

It might appear as if New Orleans is in a constant state of reconstruction.

In the summer of 1926, it rained in the Midwest—day after day after day—until the Mississippi River overflowed, causing the greatest flood the nation had seen.

The river hit flood stage at Cairo, Illinois, on New Years Day 1927, and it stayed above that level for 153 days, flooding 27,000 square miles.

Downstream, officials began to fear for the safety of New Orleans.

So they dynamited the levees downstream of New Orleans to prevent flooding in the city. However, this inundated the land to the south, ruining the lives of those residents.

The plan turned out to be unnecessary because many levees upstream had already been breached.

Hurricane Katrina, the storm that devastated New Orleans in 2005, was the sixth-largest hurricane ever recorded, and the third largest to hit the United States.

The levee system designed to protect the city failed.

About 80 percent of the city was submerged in as much as 20 feet of water.

The total number of dead, injured, homeless, and displaced may never be known.

In the period after Hurricane Katrina, the Army Corps of Engineers spent $15 billion to build a 350-mile system of locks and pumps to protect New Orleans against future storms.

Since 1956, the New Orleans metropolitan area has lost 23 percent of the natural wetlands that surrounded it.

Those wetlands are now considered to be a crucial element in the protection against hurricanes, because they slow the storms as they move up the Gulf of Mexico.

New Orleans is not always flooded.

In November 1899, the situation was quite the opposite, with no rain for four months.

Drinking water was in short supply. *The New York Times* reported that while the rich were able to buy bottled spring water, the poor were drinking the river water used to flush the streets.

Coincidentally, in the same year, the Louisiana legislature created the Sewerage and Water Board to "furnish, construct, operate, and maintain a water treatment and distribution system and a sanitary sewerage system for New Orleans."

The Board still exists today.

**W**ithin five years of the nearly total devastation caused by Hurricane Katrina, New Orleans was back on top.

Well, maybe in only one category, but it is an important one!

In May 2010, TripAdvisor.com listed New Orleans as the world's No. 1 Destination for Nightlife.

Plus, *Travel + Leisure* magazine listed the city as No. 7 on the list of Top Cities in the United States and Canada for 2010.

*Laissez les bon temps rouler!*

(That's French for "Let the good times roll!" It's a trademark phrase of the City That Care Forgot.)

In 1796, New Orleans hosted the first documented performance of an opera in North America: André Ernest Grétry's *Sylvain*. The art form has been an important part of the city's cultural life ever since.

The New Orleans Opera Association was founded in 1943, and in 2010 returned to a full-season schedule for the first time since Hurricane Katrina.

efore the arrival of Europeans, Native Americans had found a short land route from the Mississippi River to Bayou St. John, which connected to Lake Pontchartrain, providing a more direct path to the Gulf of Mexico (although they had different names for all those bodies of water, of course).

That portage from the lake to the river was significant because it dramatically simplified travel and trade.

When the French arrived, the Native Americans showed them the portage, which the French immediately decided was an excellent place for a city.

The Pontchartrain Railroad, when finished in 1831, was the second completed railroad in the country. It carried passengers and goods along the old Native American portage route between the Mississippi River (at New Orleans) and Lake Pontchartrain.

The Choctaw tribe called Lake Pontchartrain *Okwa-ta* ("wide water").

The French renamed it after the Chancellor of France, who had convinced King Louis XIV to set up a colony there.

Although the lake is only about 15 feet deep, it is 24 miles wide. With an area of about 625 square miles, it is considered to be the second-largest saltwater lake in the country, after the Great Salt Lake in Utah.

(By the way, because Lake Pontchartrain is connected to the Gulf of Mexico, it isn't really a lake. It's an estuary.)

The Lake Pontchartrain Causeway, which spans the lake, is the world's longest bridge over water (23.87 miles).

The first span was built in 1956. The second was built 80 feet away in 1969. One span is now for northbound traffic, the other for southbound. Seven crossovers are used for emergencies.

From 1794 to 1938, the Carondelet Canal connected the back edge of New Orleans to Lake Pontchartrain, providing a shipping outlet. At the end of the canal, a huge basin allowed ships to turn around for the journey back to the lake.

For a while, residents planned to build a canal to connect the basin to the Mississippi River, but it never happened.

In 1938, most of the canal, which was no longer needed, was filled in.

The extremely wide right-of-way that was going to be the connecting canal became the famed Canal Street, and Basin Street is named after the once-nearby turning basin.

The Industrial Canal, built between 1918 and 1923, finally provided a shipping route between Lake Pontchartrain and the Mississippi River, creating an important shortcut to the Gulf of Mexico.

Hurricane Katrina did substantial damage to the canal, and the issue of whether or not it should be fully restored continues to be controversial.

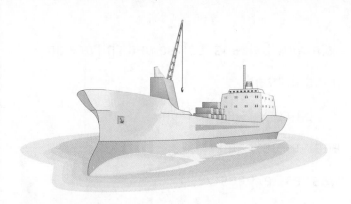

The Port of New Orleans is one of the leading general cargo ports in the country, importing more natural rubber and coffee than any other.

More than 6,000 ocean vessels move through New Orleans each year, and six of the seven top U.S. railroads provide the port with a significant distribution network.

Passenger travel is also on the rise, with more than 700,000 passengers using the gateway each year.

In New Orleans, coffee and chicory go hand in hand.

Chicory is made from endive root, and it was less expensive than coffee beans in 18th-century Europe. Adding chicory became a popular way to stretch one's coffee supply, although it does create a different taste. In New Orleans, that's considered an advantage.

Not everyone agrees, however, so in many places in the city, coffee can be had with or without.

ew Orleans played a significant role in the birth of the airline industry.

In 1912, long before airmail became a regular service, the second airmail delivery in the United States was carried from New Orleans to Baton Rouge.

French aviator George Mestach made the trip in an hour and a half. Although he hit a fence and broke his propeller while landing, he still managed to deliver the letter he was carrying to the governor.

In 1923, New Orleans was one of two U.S. cities to participate in a test program to determine whether airplanes could help speed the delivery of foreign mail.

New Orleans Air Line was formed, and seaplanes were used to carry mail back and forth from "Pilot Town" at the mouth of the Mississippi to the steamers that transported the mail to and from South America.

The trip is 85 miles on the river but only 65 miles by air. Aviation cut the time between the city mailbox and the steamer to 12 hours.

Recognizing that aviation could help promote the city, a team of business leaders in 1910 created a tournament with \$10,000 in prizes to attract the top fliers of the day.

When they arrived by train with their airplanes, the most famous of the group—John B. Moisant— took off for a breathtaking flight over the city.

He flew for 46 minutes and 10 seconds, endearing himself to the populace and breaking the world record for longest flight over a city.

Aviator René Simon made history at the weeklong New Orleans Aviation Tournament of 1910 when he broke a world record by flying one mile in 57 seconds (just over 60 miles per hour).

John Moisant, an American of French-Canadian descent, matched his plane against a Packard automobile in a five-mile race—and lost.

ohn Moisant died on New Year's Eve in 1910 while practicing for the next day's event. He crashed his plane into what later became known as the Moisant Stock Yards.

The location was approved for a commercial airport in 1940, but it didn't open until 1946, after World War II ended.

The airport was named after Moisant and received the three-letter designator MSY.

In 1960, the airport's name was changed to New Orleans International Airport, but it kept the MSY code, which can still be seen on baggage tags.

The New Orleans International Airport received a slightly longer name in August 2001, when it was renamed the Louis Armstrong New Orleans International Airport to honor the jazz musician's 100th birthday.

Known as "Satchmo," Louis Armstrong is considered one of the founding fathers of jazz, the uniquely American art form. In addition to playing the cornet and singing, the New Orleans native was a composer, writer, actor...an icon.

A tireless performer, Armstrong appeared around the world an average of 300 times a year, serving as a goodwill ambassador representing the United States in Africa, Asia, and Europe.

Louis Armstrong died at home in his sleep in 1971, less than a month shy of his 70th birthday.

New Orleans belonged to France until 1762 and the secret Treaty of Fountainebleau. The treaty was so clandestine that no one told the settlers in Louisiana.

At the time, France was not faring well in the Seven Years War with Great Britain. King Louis XV decided to give its holdings in Louisiana west of the Mississippi to Spain in exchange for its help.

France lost the war anyway and ceded all of its territory east of the Mississippi to Great Britain—but didn't reveal until 1764 that it had given New Orleans and the rest to Spain.

The French settlers resisted Spain's first attempts to assert control. The Spanish flag was not raised over the *Place d'Armes* until 1769.

The buildings in today's French Quarter are mostly of Spanish architecture.

The devastating fire of 1788, which began in the afternoon on Good Friday, burned through almost all of New Orleans within five hours.

Only a few buildings—for example, the Customs House and the Ursuline Convent—survived.

Another fire in 1794 destroyed even more.

As the city was rebuilt, the wooden structures constructed by the French were replaced with Spanish designs, including courtyards, thick brick walls, and wrought iron balconies.

In 1800, when Spain gave New Orleans back to France, the transfer once again was made by secret treaty—this one called the Third Treaty of San Ildefonso.

Again, no one told the people of New Orleans, and the French didn't even bother to take possession from the Spanish until a mere 20 days before the Louisiana Purchase was finalized in 1803.

The United States had long wanted to buy Louisiana because of its strategic importance, but Napoleon had rejected the offer. When Haiti succeeded in breaking away from France in a slave revolt, however, Napoleon's hope of extending his empire into the New World crumbled, and he was suddenly in the mood to make a deal.

The purchase agreement to transfer ownership of Louisiana from France to the United States was signed as a treaty in Paris on April 30, 1803.

The U.S. Senate ratified the treaty, approving the purchase, on October 20th.

The formal transfer of Louisiana from France to the United States finally took place on December 20th, when William C.C. Claiborne and General James Wilkinson signed the documents in the *Sala Capitular* ("Capitol meeting room") of the Cabildo building in New Orleans. (It was the same room where the French had taken possession from the Spanish on November 30th.)

The deal cost $15 million, for which the United States not only was able to secure control over the Mississippi River but also to double the size of the country—at a cost of about four cents an acre.

**G**eneral James Wilkinson, one of the two U.S. officials who executed the Louisiana Purchase, was named commander-in-chief of the U.S. forces in New Orleans and governor of the Northern Louisiana Territory.

In 1806, when Vice President Aaron Burr was accused of treason, Wilkinson declared martial law in New Orleans and began arresting suspects in the conspiracy.

Ironically, while Burr ultimately was found not guilty of conspiracy, Wilkinson turned out to be a spy.

He had pledged his allegiance to the King of Spain on a trip to visit the Spanish governor of New Orleans in 1787.

Wilkinson secretly received payments from Spain for many years.

**I**f Napoleon Bonaparte had chosen to leave his exile in Elba, he had a home waiting for him in New Orleans.

In 1821, Nicholas Girod, who had been mayor of New Orleans from 1812 to 1815, publicly offered to provide shelter for the ex-emperor.

Napoleon never showed up, but the offer is immortalized in the name of the building, now known as the Napoleon House.

Today, it is one of the quintessential New Orleans bars, famous for (among other things) a drink called a Pimm's Cup—made of Pimm's No. 1 (a digestif), lemonade, 7-Up, and cucumbers.

After all it's been through, New Orleans deserves a drink.

And now, it officially has one of its own.

The Louisiana Legislature named the Sazerac the official cocktail of New Orleans in 2008.

The Sazerac was invented in the 1830s by a Creole pharmacist named Antoine Peychaud. His original recipe involved cognac, absinthe, and Peychaud's own secret blend of bitters.

Today, rye whiskey is substituted for cognac, and Herbsaint stands in for absinthe.

Peychaud's bitters, however, are an irreplaceable ingredient.

The Sazerac certainly was not the first alcoholic drink ever served, but it was apparently the first "cocktail."

When Antoine Peychaud (and the bartenders who followed him)  made a Sazerac, he used an eggcup as his measuring tool.

The French word for the eggcup is *coquetier*, which, when Anglicized, evolved into the word "cocktail."

In the 1880s, Henry C. Ramos was on his way to becoming the most famous mixologist of the South. Ramos owned a saloon in the French Quarter, and he came up with a gin drink made with citrus juices, egg whites, sugar, cream, some additional flavors...and a healthy shaking arm.

Some say the drink—the Ramos Gin Fizz—must be shaken for as many as 12 minutes before serving, and the bar had a row of shaker boys dedicated to the task.

Ramos served this incredibly popular drink until Prohibition stopped him. Then he published his secret recipe.

Today, the Sazerac Bar and Restaurant in the Roosevelt Hotel is the place to go for the official Ramos Gin Fizz.

One of the few remaining buildings from the original French Quarter (before the fires of 1788 and 1794) is Lafitte's Blacksmith Shop.

Jean Lafitte and his brother were said to operate the shop as a front for the more profitable business of being a pirate.

Today, the building houses a pub.

The last battle of the War of 1812 was for New Orleans, a strategic target that would have given the British control of the Mississippi River.

General Andrew Jackson arrived to protect the city in December 1814. During the next few weeks, he assembled a patchwork military force that included militia from Louisiana and surrounding regions, free men of color, slaves, and even pirates.

Jean Lafitte, the legendary pirate leader, had been approached by the British to join them. Instead, he negotiated with the Americans for amnesty for himself and his men in exchange for their support in battle.

By year's end, the war officially had ended with an American victory and the signing of the Treaty of Ghent. It would be weeks before anyone in New Orleans knew.

On January 8, 1815, thousands of British massed for an attack in Chalmette, near New Orleans, unaware that the war was officially over.

General Andrew Jackson, who also didn't know that a treaty had been signed, had his troops dig trenches and wait for the British to arrive.

As the British troops marched in firing range, Jackson's forces mowed them down, row after row, until they surrendered.

More than 2,000 British were killed. Jackson lost 71 men.

Arsène LaCarrière Latour is credited with choosing the spot where General Andrew Jackson's troops built their earthen encampment, waiting for the British in the Battle of New Orleans.

Latour was an architect when he wasn't a battle-time army engineer. In addition to designing and building houses, Latour was chosen to replace the original French Market building with something more ornate. His structure, completed in 1811, was completely destroyed in a hurricane the following year. (Is anyone noticing a pattern here?)

$\mathcal{S}$laves were imported to New Orleans as early as 1717 to begin draining the swamps and building the levees.

Throughout the 18th century, the slaves outnumbered the white settlers.

The *Code Noir* (Black Code) was a set of laws incorporating punishments so severe for disobedience that a small number of landowners could control a large population of slaves.

In the early 19th century, New Orleans was dependent on a trade economy, and the two biggest trading items were cotton and slaves.

By the middle of the century, New Orleans had the biggest slave market in the country.

In April 1862, U.S. naval forces came up the Mississippi River and captured New Orleans, the largest city in the Confederacy, without a shot being fired.

Thirteen months after Louisiana joined the Confederate States of America at the start of the Civil War, New Orleans was back under federal control.

The city remained under occupation until the end of the war, and all its historic architecture remained intact.

In the days before New Orleans was captured from the Confederacy in April 1862, two U.S. Marines came ashore and raised the Stars and Stripes over the Mint Building.

William Mumford, along with several other New Orleans residents, tore the flag down.

After New Orleans' surrender, Union Army Major General Benjamin Butler charged Mumford with treason. Mumford claimed his actions were legal under Confederate law, which he said should have applied at the time, because the city hadn't yet been captured.

Mumford's argument fell on deaf ears, and he was executed on June 7th.

Confederate President Jefferson Davis responded to the news by calling for the execution of Butler if he were ever captured.

He wasn't.

Few things inspired as much outrage in New Orleans as an order issued in 1862. It sought to protect Union soldiers from women who were spitting at, verbally abusing, and even emptying chamber pots upon them:

As the officers and soldiers of the United States have been subject to repeated insults from the women (calling themselves ladies) of New Orleans in return for the most scrupulous non-interference and courtesy on our part, it is ordered that hereafter when any female shall by word, gesture, or movement insult or show contempt for any officer or soldier of the United States, she shall be regarded and held liable to be treated as a woman of the town plying her avocation.

It worked.

The U.S. Mint in New Orleans is recognized as the only place where coins were struck for both the United States and the Confederate States of America.

Although that's true, it's a bit of a stretch.

When Louisiana seceded from the Union in January 1861, it took possession of the mint and the half million dollars in gold and silver stored there.

After Louisiana joined the Confederacy, the Confederate government took possession of the mint on April 1st.

That month, a Confederate half-dollar coin was designed, and four coins were produced in a test run.

On April 30th, due to a lack of bullion, the Confederate mint ceased operations.

Three of those four coins belong to private collectors. The fourth is in the American Numismatic Society collection in New York City.

In 1862, when U.S. Marines entered and occupied New Orleans, possession of the mint was returned to the federal government. U.S. coins were produced there again starting in 1879. In 1909, it no longer was cost effective to continue using the facility, and the mint was closed.

After 1910, the federal government used the building as an assay office and a prison and ultimately gave it to Louisiana to use as a museum, which currently is open to the public.

$\mathcal{J}$udah Benjamin settled in New Orleans in the 1830s, became a lawyer, and in 1853 became the first openly Jewish senator in the U.S. Congress. He is said to have been offered a nomination to the Supreme Court twice, but turned it down.

In 1861, after Louisiana seceded from the Union, Benjamin resigned from the Senate.

Under Jefferson Davis, he served in the Confederate States of America government as Secretary of War and Secretary of State, thereby becoming the first Jewish cabinet-level politician in North America.

At the end of the Civil War, he moved to Great Britain, where he had an illustrious career in the practice of law.

ST. JOHN THE BAPTIST PARISH LIBRARY
2920 NEW HIGHWAY 51
LAPLACE, LOUISIANA 70068

**101**
NEW ORLEANS
FACTS

In 1866, the U.S. Congress established the first regiment of Buffalo Soldiers, and New Orleans was the first place where the new colored cavalry were recruited.

There was little difficulty in filling the positions with freed slaves and free men of color.

The 9th Regiment, as it officially was called, went on to play an important role in the taming of the West, fighting Indians and escorting wagon trains.

The city of New Orleans is home to Louisiana's Civil War Museum at Confederate Memorial Hall and the National World War II Museum.

The "Confederate Museum" is the state's largest museum and houses one of the nation's biggest collections of Civil War-era artifacts from the South. It opened in 1891, assuring that future generations would remember the contributions made by veterans of the War Between the States.

The National D-Day Museum opened in June 2000, received its designation from Congress as the country's official museum of World War II in 2003, and reopened as the National World War II Museum in 2006.

That museum's oral history project features interviews from World War II veterans to preserve their stories.

The only statue dedicated to the Marines in New Orleans is of a woman.

Built in 1943 and standing at the intersection of Canal and Elk streets, the sculpture named "Molly Marine" was erected in an effort to recruit women during World War II.

She stands gazing into the sky, presumably watching for enemy fighter planes, while the caption below her reads, "Free a Marine to Fight."

Molly is the first statue ever erected of a United States female service member in uniform and is still considered an important symbol to women in the corps.

The Marines have erected copies of the statue on bases at Parris Island, South Carolina, and Quantico, Virginia.

New Orleans was the home of the man Adolph Hitler called the "New Noah."

Andrew Higgins developed and built the landing craft that transported Allied forces during the World War II Invasion of Normandy.

Twenty thousand of what the military called the Landing Craft, Vehicle, Personnel were built by Higgins Industries.

Thirty-six men could be transported in the iconic Higgins boat.

When it reached shore, the front of the boat was lowered to provide a ramp exit for the soldiers to storm the beach.

General Dwight D. Eisenhower credited Higgins and his boat with winning the war.

New Orleans served as the official Louisiana state capital until 1849, when Baton Rouge took its place.

When the Civil War ended in 1865, New Orleans reclaimed its title until 1880, when Baton Rouge picked up the baton again.

At 170 feet, Canal Street is the widest street in New Orleans, if not the world.

It has three lanes of traffic in each direction and a series of streetcar tracks in between.

For nearly a century, Canal Street was the retailing center of town, with department stores, specialty shops, and what is in retrospect billed as the world's first movie theater.

During the second half of the 20th century, shoppers took their business to the suburbs, while convention hotels took their place along Canal Street.

Today, luxury apartments and tourist attractions dot this street that divides the French Quarter from the American Sector.

When Louisiana became part of the United States and northerners started moving to New Orleans, the Creoles were not glad to see them.

With their French and Spanish heritage, the Creoles found Americans to be unpolished and lacking in class.

Canal Street, which had a park-like median with grass and trees, effectively became the border between the French Quarter and the American Sector.

As an indication of just how much the two groups didn't get along, the cross streets were given different names as they left the French Quarter. For example, *Rue Chartres* becomes Camp Street.

Even more telling: The median became known as "neutral ground," and all medians in New Orleans are still referred to that way today.

**L**ouisiana voodoo is, on one hand, an amalgam of spiritual beliefs and cultural practices brought from Africa by slaves. On the other hand, the practice has incorporated some of the rites and rituals of Roman Catholicism, which was enforced as the "true religion" of New Orleans during its colonial period.

Marked by its use of herbs and poisons, charms and amulets, and incantations to spirits, voodoo was practiced among the Creoles through mediums thought to have mystic power.

Marie Laveau is remembered as the strongest of such voodoo queens.

**M**arie Laveau was born near the start of the 19th century, the daughter of two free persons of color.

She married young and had two children who died early.

Her husband either died or left, and Marie began calling herself a widow.

She took a lover by *plaçage* and had many more children.

Marie became a hairdresser in the French Quarter, learning many of her customers' secrets, a powerful weapon in a class-conscious society.

Although Marie professed to be a devout Catholic, stories abound of her performing mystical ceremonies and incantations.

Her integrity has always been a matter of debate, with some claiming she was a charlatan and others believing in her spirituality.

**M**arie Laveau died in 1881 and was buried in St. Louis Cemetery No. 1.

As might be expected of a voodoo queen, however, Marie's story did not end with her death.

She had a daughter, who also went by the name of Marie Laveau, and who was said to look very much like her mother.

Toward the end of the elder Marie's life, Marie II joined in the family practice. The daughter marketed the occult powers her mother was said to have had and turned them into a profitable business.

When Marie I died, Marie II took over. She was said to look enough like her mother that believers assumed the original queen of voodoo had never died.

111

NEW ORLEANS
FACTS

For anyone interested in learning more about voodoo, whether from an academic or a more personal perspective, the Voodoo Museum stands ready to serve.

Located in the French Quarter since 1972, the museum has experts who educate, tour guides who lead walking tours through the city, "readers" who can commune with the spirits, and a gift shop where visitors can obtain the raw materials for magic and mischief (or, for the less adventurous, just a T-shirt).

Wall Street in the French Quarter?

Not exactly, but there was a time (1835 to 1842, to be exact) when New Orleans had more banking capital than New York City.

While other states were feeling the roller coaster ride of the economy, banking in Louisiana offered a strong sense of stability. The state's Bank Act of 1842 required banks to maintain a gold or silver reserve against notes and deposits. It was the first such regulation in the United States.

In the early 1870s, sediment brought downstream by the Mississippi River current was clogging the shipping channels.

With dredging proving only nominally helpful, the U.S. Army Corps of Engineers in 1874 recommended building a canal between the city and the Gulf.

James Eads, a well-known and accomplished engineer, suggested letting the river dredge itself. Building walls to funnel the flow of the river into a narrower channel, he said, would make the water flow faster and push the sediment out to sea.

To counter the objections of skeptics, Eads offered to do the job without getting paid unless his plan worked.

Within five years, a permanent 30-foot channel provided year-round access to New Orleans, and Eads earned $4.25 million.

Because most of New Orleans is below sea level, the city relies on a drainage system that can lift water above the levees and dump it into the Mississippi.

Until the beginning of the 20th century, the methods used for draining New Orleans were truly inadequate, and a lack of public funding had prevented any progress from being made.

A. Baldwin Wood, a New Orleans native, used his engineering skills and inventive mind to create innovative solutions that transformed the science of pumping water.

Wood's "flapgates" prevented water from backing up when the pumps were turned off. The Wood Screw Pumps, invented in 1913, performed best when they were needed most—in times of flooding.

In 1867, during a yellow fever epidemic, a Catholic priest in the *Faubourg* Franklin neighborhood turned for help to St. Roch, patron saint of plague victims. The priest promised that if no one in his parish died, he would dedicate a chapel to the saint.

Everyone in his congregation lived, and the priest kept his word. He built not only a chapel, but also a cemetery, called Campo Santo, to honor St. Roch.

Construction was finished in 1876, and the next yellow fever epidemic hit in 1878. No one in the parish died then, either.

oday, the *Faubourg* Franklin neighborhood is called St. Roch.

In the years since the chapel was built, people have come seeking relief from a variety of physical ailments. A room off the chapel is filled with offerings of items like crutches, glass eyeballs, and false limbs— thanks from people who apparently no longer needed them and testaments to their successful supplications to St. Roch.

St. Roch Cathedral is the destination for young women in search of a husband.

Legend has it that offering a prayer at nine different churches on Good Friday will assure a woman of being married within a year.

It is said that women who offer up their ninth prayer at St. Roch will double their luck.

New Orleans is famous not just for how it treats the living but for how it handles its dead. Because the city is below sea level, burying people underground is neither easy nor a good idea, so most burial sites in New Orleans are in above-ground tombs.

That provides the added advantage of being able to reuse the same burial site more than once, because the bodies decompose relatively quickly in the hot, humid climate.

The cemeteries, with all the tombs looking like little houses, are sometimes referred to as Cities of the Dead.

New Orleans has 31 historic cemeteries, and the city views them with pride. Each is distinct, representing different ethnic cultures and religious backgrounds.

St. Louis No. 1, a Roman Catholic cemetery, opened in 1789 near the French Quarter and is the oldest still in existence.

Although it covers only a one-block area, more than 100,000 people have been buried there.

St. Louis Cemetery No. 2 opened in 1823, about three blocks away from the first St. Louis cemetery.

The newer cemetery is about three times the size of the first and is ornately decorated with ironwork.

Many blues and jazz musicians are buried in St. Louis No. 2, along with other notable figures from New Orleans history.

Defying convention, Holt Cemetery has a majority of in-ground burials. It was established in 1879, providing a lower-cost alternative to other sites. Instead of paying to build a tomb, a family would get the right to use a piece of land as a burial site as long as they maintained the grave.

When Hurricane Katrina flooded Holt, many of the graves were damaged, and some bones were exposed.

In 1974, when a development project included the planned demolition of nine city blocks of wall vaults in St. Louis Cemetery No. 2, Save Our Cemeteries was founded. The organization has since expanded to include the protection of all the historic cemeteries of New Orleans and the rest of Louisiana.

Its fundamental goals are restoration, preservation, and education.

**H**enriette DeLille, buried at St. Louis Cemetery No. 2, may be destined for sainthood.

Born to a financially secure family in 1813, she was a free woman of color who refused to pass as white in order to advance in society.

DeLille, a Catholic, wanted to be a nun, but her color prevented her from joining any existing religious community. Determined to dedicate her life to the service of slaves and poor people of color, she began a religious community of her own.

By 1842, the Sisters of the Holy Family had been recognized by the Vatican, and it is still active today with more than 200 members.

In March 2010, the Venerable Mother Henriette received the blessing of Pope Benedict XVI.

New Orleans' Ursuline Academy, founded in 1727, is the oldest continuously operating school for women and the oldest Catholic school in the United States.

Sisters of the Order of Saint Ursula taught the daughters of Native Americans, Africans, and European settlers.

In 1734, an Ursuline convent and school was built on *Rue Chartres*.

In 1752, a second convent replaced the first in the same location. That structure is said to be the oldest building in the Mississippi Valley. It became the residence of the Bishop of New Orleans in the 1820s.

The nuns moved from the Old Ursuline Convent to a new location on the Mississippi. That convent was destroyed in the 1910s to make way for the Industrial Canal. Today the Ursuline Sisters live in a convent on State Street.

The National Park Service calls the Old Ursuline Convent "the finest surviving example of French colonial public architecture in the country."

From 1827 to 1829, and then again in 1831, the Louisiana Legislature met in the building while it tried to find a more permanent abode.

Today, the bottom floor is a museum, and the archdiocese historic library is kept upstairs.

The magnolia is the state flower of Louisiana, but Hurricane Katrina apparently didn't get the memo.

It's estimated that every magnolia tree in two-thirds of the city was destroyed by the storm.

The Sacred Heart Courtyard and Mausoleum at Ursuline Academy lost all of its magnolia trees and the cedar trees that had been there for almost 100 years.

In City Park alone, more than 2,000 trees were killed by Hurricane Katrina, including oaks, magnolias, pines, and palms.

In the years since then, park officials have been replanting with the help of federal money and private donations.

For a $750 donation, City Park will plant a tree and maintain it for a year to get it started. The donor receives the GPS coordinates of the tree and recognition on a donor wall in the Casino Building.

NEW ORLEANS
FACTS

With all the abandoned sites and salvageable material available around New Orleans after Hurricane Katrina, how could anyone resist pulling it all together to build a giant tree house?

At 1614 Esplanade Avenue, in the NOLA Art House, a group called HomeMade Parachutes has built a five-story tree house in a golden rain tree.

The structure has a rope bridge, a canopy lookout tower, a waterslide—all the comforts of home.

Moreover, it's a work that is continually in progress, so who knows when it also will have hot and cold running water, WiFi Internet access, and satellite television!

City Park is the site of the premier celebration of the Christmas season in New Orleans. The park is said to hold one of the largest collections of mature oaks in the world, and these trees are decorated with lights as part of the Celebration in the Oaks.

The display opens on the day after Thanksgiving and continues until early January.

City Park is also home to a carousel from 1906 and the Sydney and Walda Besthoff Sculpture Garden, covering nearly five acres with 57 sculptures.

For many years, a duel was a legal and honorable method for settling disputes in New Orleans. More duels were fought here than in any other American city.

Disputes need not have been terribly serious to warrant a duel; they only needed to have the scent of personal honor at stake.

One of the most common locations for the *affaires d'honneur* was the Duelling Oaks in City Park. During the heyday of the face-slapping challenges, the park saw at least one duel a day. Some days, as many as 10 pairs of men awaited a turn to settle a score.

By 1890, duels had fallen out of favor.

Today, only one of the two landmark oak trees remains.

Homer Plessy was an octoroon. He had one black and seven white great-grandparents. In Louisiana in the 1890s, being one-eighth black made him colored and therefore prohibited from using whites-only facilities.

As a challenge to the state law, Plessy bought a train ticket, boarded a whites-only car, and announced that he had a black great-grandparent. He was arrested.

Plessy took his case to the U.S. Supreme Court, which decided against him in 1896, ruling that blacks could be required by law to use separate facilities from whites, as long as the facilities were of equal quality. This doctrine of "separate, but equal" was used as a basis for segregation in the United States until 1953.

Homer Plessy is buried in St. Louis No. 1.

The landmark 1896 Supreme Court decision approving segregation is called Plessy v. Ferguson, because the name of the original judge before whom the case was brought was John Howard Ferguson.

Judge Ferguson is buried in Lafayette Cemetery in New Orleans.

Following the Civil War, New Orleans was the only southern city where whites and blacks attended the same schools.

The *New Orleans Tribune* wrote in 1867 of segregated schools, "Separation is not equality. The very assignment of certain schools to certain children on the ground of color is a distinction violative of the first principles of equality."

The integration of the schools didn't last past Reconstruction, however, falling to white opposition soon after northern troops returned control of internal affairs to local governments.

In 1960, New Orleans was once again the front line in the battle for school desegregation.

By order of a federal judge, four black children were sent to attend previously all-white elementary schools. Three of the children attended the same school, while one first-grader, Ruby Bridge, went to William Frantz Public School alone—except for the federal marshals who protected her and the angry white mob that cursed her. (Ruby's walk to school was immortalized in the Norman Rockwell painting, "The Problem We All Live With," in 1964.)

Ruby wound up in a classroom of her own, being taught by a white teacher from Boston.

By second grade, no one protested when she and other black children attended the first day of school at William Frantz.

John McDonogh was a businessman who moved to New Orleans at the beginning of the 19th century. He died in 1850 with no heirs, leaving two million dollars to be divided equally between New Orleans and Baltimore, his hometown, for the benefit of the public education for white and free black children.

In a memo to his executors, McDonogh explained that he believed New Orleans would be "one of the greatest [cities] in extent and population the world has ever seen." He spent the last 40 years of his life amassing as much money as possible to establish an endowment for education that would "become in time a huge mountain of wealth...and the benefit of Generations yet unborn."

By the time John McDonogh's estate had made its way through the courts, about $700,000 dollars was left for New Orleans. That was enough to build more than 30 schools, which were labeled with his name and a number. For example, one of the first two elementary schools to be integrated by court order in the 1950s was "McDonogh No. 19."

Toward the end of the 20th century, in an effort to remove the names of slaveholders from the New Orleans public schools, many of the McDonogh schools were redesignated. For example, McDonogh No. 19 became Louis Armstrong Elementary.

Nevertheless, there are still seven McDonogh schools today.

The last of John McDonogh's endowment for New Orleans education was spent in 2002, but his legacy continues.

McDonogh asked that students place flowers around his grave annually, but his remains were moved to Baltimore in 1860.

From 1892 to 1898, school children of New Orleans saved their pennies to erect a monument to McDonogh in Lafayette Square. From 1898 to the 1950s, the children paid their respects to him there annually on McDonogh Day. The practice has fallen out of favor, and only one school still celebrates the day.

In 2010, the children of New Orleans' McDonogh No. 26 gathered at the McDonogh memorial in McDonoghville cemetery on May 7th for the 120th annual McDonogh Day ceremony.

In December 1884, as part of its continuing effort to spur tourism and investment after the Civil War, the city of New Orleans hosted the World's Industrial and Cotton Centennial Exposition.

The World's Fair commemorated the 100th anniversary of the city's first cotton exports.

The area known today as Audubon Park was the site of the fair and a building that, at nearly two million square feet, was the largest wooden structure ever built.

Nearly all the structures built for the fair were torn down by the end of the 19th century.

One hundred years after the World's Industrial and Cotton Centennial Exposition, New Orleans hosted another World's Fair.

Twenty-one countries participated in the 1984 exposition, but the event was not financially successful.

In fact, it was the first World's Fair to declare bankruptcy and the last such event to be hosted in the United States.

Nevertheless, the 1984 New Orleans World's Fair is remembered fondly by many locals and is credited with bringing a convention center to the city.

The architect who transformed the site of the 1884 World's Industrial and Cotton Centennial Exposition was John Charles Olmsted, whose family firm also designed New York's Central Park.

The area's name was changed from Upper City Park to Audubon Park in recognition of naturalist John James Audubon, who had painted many of his *Birds of America* in Louisiana.

The park includes a 1.8-mile paved walking path and a number of outdoor sports facilities for the public.

The Audubon Zoo traces its roots back to 1916, when a flight cage was added to Audubon Park.

Little by little, using private funds and money from the Works Progress Administration during the Depression, a zoo took shape—first with the addition of a monkey cage, later an elephant, and ultimately an aquarium with a sea lion pool.

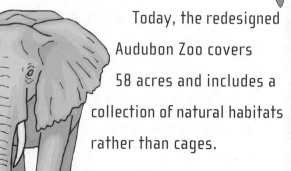

Today, the redesigned Audubon Zoo covers 58 acres and includes a collection of natural habitats rather than cages.

The Audubon Aquarium opened in 1990 in Woldenberg Park along the Mississippi riverfront.

Since then, the Audubon attractions in New Orleans have continued to grow under the umbrella of the Audubon Nature Institute.

The institute's facilities house a unique species survival center, which includes a "Frozen Zoo," preserving the genetic material of hundreds of threatened species.

The most recent Audubon addition  in New Orleans is the Insectarium, which opened in 2008.

Located in the historic U.S. Custom House, it is the  largest freestanding museum in the United States dedicated to insects.

The Warehouse District of New Orleans was, as the name might suggest, an industrial-size storage area where products shipped through the Port of New Orleans were held between journeys.

Today, that neighborhood is the New Orleans Arts District, replete with galleries, museums, and restaurants.

The transformation began in 1976 with the construction of the Contemporary Arts Center and continued during the 1984 World's Fair.

Julia Street is the heart of the New Orleans Arts District, with a string of galleries that attract tourists and natives.

The 600 block of Julia Street is lined by a row of 13 side-by-side townhouses built in 1833.

The Thirteen Sisters, as the townhouses are called, were the first homes of that type of construction in New Orleans.

Although the narrow lots and shared walls were more common in northern cities like Baltimore and Philadelphia, they turned out to be popular among the affluent of that era in New Orleans, too.

A gallery-hopping event called the Art Walk is hosted by the galleries of the New Orleans Arts District on the first Saturday evening of each month.

The first Saturday in August is known as Whitney White Linen Night, featuring a combination of food, drink, music, and art.

The following Saturday, Dirty Linen Night on Royal Street, allows budget-conscious linen wearers to save on their laundry bills.

The largest art walk of the year is Art for Arts' Sake, sponsored by the Contemporary Arts Center on the first Saturday of October. It draws 30,000 visitors annually.

The New Orleans Arts District is a Louisiana Cultural District, so original works of art sold there are not subject to sales tax.

In the early days of New Orleans, Bayou St. John provided access by water to the city. It was a popular place for residences among the well-to-do during the French and Spanish colonial eras, but only one of those stately homes still exists today: the Pitot House.

James Pitot was the first American mayor of New Orleans (after the Louisiana Purchase), and he owned the home from 1810 to 1819. The Creole colonial-style building has been restored to its historic condition and furnished with 19th-century antiques. It is now open to the public as a museum.

The Pitot House Museum is also the headquarters of the Louisiana Landmarks Society.

One of the few remaining structures in the French Quarter after the 1794 fire is now known as Madame John's Legacy.

Built after the earlier catastrophic fire of 1788, this structure is typical of the homes belonging to the prosperous Louisiana Creoles of the time.

In addition to the main house, Madame John's Legacy has a kitchen with cook's quarters and a separate two-story apartment.

The home is elevated to circumvent frequent flooding, and a courtyard connects the buildings.

The site is open to the public, and it is listed as a National Historic Landmark.

The 1789 structure known as Madame John's Legacy got its name at the intersection of truth and fiction.

George Washington Cable, a contemporary of Mark Twain, wrote a short story based in and around the residence in 1883, when it was already nearly 100 years old.

*'Tite Poulette* is a story of the class structure of the time. Madame John, a Creole character in the story, becomes the owner of the old residence after the previous owner bequeaths it to her on his deathbed.

The character, rather than the owner of the building in real life, is now remembered as the source of this historical remnant of the French Quarter.

nne Rice, the noted author of *Interview with the Vampire* and *The Feast of All Saints*, is a New Orleans native.

"Anne" was not the name she was born with, though. She was originally Howard Allen O'Brien, named after her father.

Howard took matters into her own hands when she entered the first grade at St. Alphonsus Grammar School, however. When the teacher asked her name on the first day of school, Howard said, "Anne," and that was that.

Anne attended Catholic school in New Orleans until 1958, when her family moved to Texas.

The home at the corner of First and Chestnut Streets is the inspiration for Mayfair Manor, the home of Anne Rice's Mayfair Witches.

The structure at 1239 First Street was built in 1857 for Albert Hamilton Brevard, a wealthy merchant.

Anne Rice, a native of New Orleans, lived in the home with her husband from 1989 to 2004.

When author William Faulkner lived in New Orleans in the 1920s, his home was a small, four-story boarding house in the French Quarter, which then was a slum.

Within a year of arriving in New Orleans, Faulkner had written and published *Soldier's Pay*, his first novel. The New Orleans influence can be seen in his later novels, *Mosquitoes*, *The Wild Palms*, and *Absalom! Absalom!*

Today, the ground floor of the building where he lived is home of Faulkner House Books, a small shop on what is now called Pirates Alley.

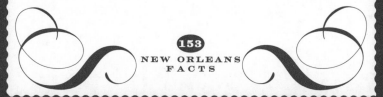

Playwright Tennessee Williams lived in New Orleans in the 1940s.

His first apartment was at 722 Toulouse Street, but he was living at 632 St. Peter Street when he wrote his Pulitzer-Prize-winning play, *A Streetcar Named Desire*, set on Elysian Fields Avenue in the *Faubourg Marigny* section of the city.

The Desire streetcar was replaced with a bus line in 1948, shortly after the play was written.

When New Orleans opened the St. Charles streetcar line in 1835, it became the second city in America to start streetcar service. (New York's Bowery Line opened a few years earlier.) Today, the St. Charles line is the oldest continuously operating streetcar in the world.

The St. Charles line runs from the French Quarter uptown through the Garden District, where the Americans settled after the Louisiana Purchase.

In the early days, horses pulled the streetcars along their tracks, but electricity has been doing the job since just before the turn of the 20th century.

At one point, New Orleans had 235 miles of streetcar tracks until buses began to replace them.

Today, the streetcars of the St. Charles line in New Orleans are listed on the National Park Service's Register of Historic Places.

Rarely can a single historic landmark offer the two-for-one value of the Beauregard-Keyes House. Built in 1826, this building on *Rue Chartres* was, at different times in history, the home of both Confederate General P.G.T. Beauregard and author Frances Parkinson Keyes.

Beauregard, a New Orleans native, was the general who ordered the opening shots of the Civil War, which were fired on Fort Sumter in April 1861. After the war, he was president of the New Orleans, Jackson & Great Northern Railroad, and he lived in this French Quarter home from 1866 to 1868.

Keyes wrote many of her books (*Dinner at Antoine's, The Chess Players,* and *Blue Camellia*) in the residence from the 1950s to 1970.

Edgar Degas, the famous French impressionist painter, spent a year with his mother's family in New Orleans from 1872 to 1873. During his visit, he painted 22 canvases of his family members, including *A Cotton Office*, which was the only Degas work that was purchased by a museum during his lifetime.

Today, the home and studio where he painted in New Orleans is open to the public.

Built in 1852, the house is now furnished with period pieces and copies of Degas' paintings.

Seven guest rooms are available to the public for overnight stays.

In 1886, Antonio Monteleone, a Sicilian cobbler, bought a 64-room hotel on Royal Street in the French Quarter. Today, the hotel, which is still run by the Monteleone family, is one of only three hotels ever to be designated a literary landmark by the Friends of the Library Association. (New York's Plaza and Algonquin are the others.)

Ernest Hemingway and Tennessee Williams were regulars.

William Faulkner and Eudora Welty used the hotel as a setting in their stories.

Truman Capote's mother lived there when he was born, which prompted him to boast that he had been born in the Hotel Monteleone.

Chefs Emeril Lagasse and Paul Prudhomme are New Orleans' own, but they're new kids on the block when it comes to the city's historic cuisine.

For a traditional meal on a budget, the Po-Boy is the gold standard.

In the 1920s, Clovis and Benjamin Martin left their jobs as streetcar drivers to start a restaurant. When their former colleagues went on strike in 1929, the Martin brothers supported the cause with an inexpensive sandwich of roast beef bits and gravy.

Legend has it that every time a striking worker came in for a sandwich, the kitchen workers called out, "Here comes another poor boy!" The name stuck, and now it refers to a variety of over-stuffed sandwiches available around town.

In colonial times, saffron was a prohibitively expensive spice in New Orleans, but it was an essential element of the Spanish dish *paella*.

Using available spices from the Caribbean and adding tomatoes to the mix, resourceful chefs of the day wound up inventing *jambalaya*.

There are many conflicting theories about the origin of the word, but regardless of its beginnings, the word has come to reflect the nature of the dish—a tasty concoction of whatever ingredients one has on hand.

Long before the Europeans arrived, Native Americans were catching and eating and enjoying crawfish, the crustacean native to Louisiana waters.

For centuries, the crawfish has been a plentiful and popular food source on the palette of New Orleans' chefs.

In the 1960s, researchers figured out how to farm crawfish, and today the annual harvest in Louisiana can top 100 million pounds, which amounts to 90 percent of the U.S. domestic output.

**B**irthday cake is something any city can provide, but Doberge cake is unique to New Orleans.

With six-plus thin layers of cake separated by dessert pudding (usually half lemon and half chocolate), the recipe is an adaptation of the Dobos cake from Hungary. It is covered with butter cream and a light shell or glaze.

Beulah Ledner created the Doberge cake in the 1930s. The recipe was included in a cookbook released by her daughter in 1987: *Let's Bake with Beulah Ledner: A Legendary New Orleans Lady*.

By now, it should be clear how any mundane exercise can be New-Orleanized: Add food, alcohol, and music; extend it beyond any measure of moderation; put it on a regular schedule; and enjoy it with reckless abandon.

At Galatoire's, a century-plus-old restaurant in the French Quarter, the Friday lunch has become just such a legendary experience.

Although it is sometimes necessary to spend a few hours on the sidewalk to get a table, Friday lunch at Galatoire's begins (routinely enough) on Friday around lunchtime, but it doesn't end until late Friday night.

In between, well, it's just a party—with food, drinks, and laughter in an old-world atmosphere that shows no interest in catching up with the times.

**M**any religions serve huge meals to break a fast and begin the celebration of a particular holiday.

Leave it to New Orleans to do away with the fast, keep the feast, and schedule it for every night of the week.

That's what happened with the *réveillon*. Literally translated as "awakening," the meal was traditionally served after midnight mass on Christmas Eve and was a family affair of eggs, soups, oysters, veal, etc.

Common in the 19th century, the *réveillon* had all but disappeared by the 1940s. Then, 50 years later, the tourist industry revived it as a draw for visitors every night during the usually quiet holiday season.

Now the *réveillion* menu is just another opportunity to eat, drink, and be merry.

New Orleans
is the murder capital
of the United States, with
174 murders in 2009—a
rate of about 52 people
per 100,000.

La Salle (French explorer Robert Cavelier) claimed Louisiana for France.

France gave it to Spain, then took it back.

The United States bought it from France.

So when did all the Greeks get there?

The Hellenic community took root in New Orleans during the 19th century, and the first Greek Orthodox Church in the Western Hemisphere was founded there in 1860.

Today's Holy Trinity Cathedral is the successor of that church, and the Annual Greek Festival—"Greece on the Bayou"—has been going strong since 1974.

Tulane University was founded in 1834 as the Medical College of Louisiana.

In 1845, it was designated the University of Louisiana, but there were never enough public funds to run the school well.

In the 1880s, philanthropist Paul Tulane made it possible for the school to go private, and today it carries his name.

Like most top universities Tulane has a long list of achievements that recommend it to prospective students.

Tulane received more applications in 2010 than any other U.S. university, so the list is clearly impressive.

Tulane's boasts and brags from its website include: The auditorium is "the world's largest self-suspended concrete dome," the law school is the 12th oldest in the country, the library has a leaf from the Gutenberg Bible, and the stadium has hosted the Super Bowl.

Another bonus, however, has a unique New Orleans flair:

"Stored beneath the bleachers in Tulane Stadium for 24 years, mummies Got Thothi Aunk and Nefer Atethu are the only Egyptians from 900 B.C. to attend the Super Bowl."

The first commencement address to Tulane's Medical School graduates in 1836 was given in Latin by the dean.

In 2009, when the class that entered immediately after Hurricane Katrina graduated, New Orleans native Ellen DeGeneres gave the commencement address.

She urged the students to live lives of integrity and to avoid giving in to peer pressure.

Although she recommended that they neither give nor take any advice, she offered this sage advice:

"Follow your passion. Stay true to yourself. Never follow anyone else's path unless you're in the woods, and you're lost, and you see a path, and by all means you should follow that."

Lee Harvey Oswald was a native of New Orleans.

He went to Beauregard Junior High and Warren Easton High schools.

On August 21, 1963, radio listeners were treated to an interview with Oswald, who was the secretary of the New Orleans chapter of the Fair Play for Cuba Committee, an organization based in New York.

Although one might have thought at the time that he had used up his 15 minutes of fame with that appearance, Oswald immortalized himself barely three months later in Dallas with the assassination of President John F. Kennedy.

Warren Easton High School suffered more than $4 million dollars in damage during Hurricane Katrina.

Academy Award-winner Sandra Bullock lent her celebrity status to help raise the funds necessary to rebuild the school.

On the fifth anniversary of the storm, Warren Easton opened its own full-service medical and dental clinic on campus.

Warren Easton, now a charter high school, has a nearly 100 percent graduation rate.

ew Orleans is home to the oldest black neighborhood in America— the *Faubourg Tremé*, named after Claude Tremé, who emigrated to New Orleans in 1783 and owned property in the area.

The neighborhood is home to the Backstreet Cultural Museum, which houses costumes of the *Mardi Gras* Indians; the Louisiana Museum of African American History; the New Orleans African American Museum; St. Louis Cemetery No. 1; and Louis Armstrong Park, which includes historic Congo Square.

As early as the 18th century, Congo Square was a weekly meeting place for slaves and free people of color, who gathered on Sundays to trade goods, to socialize, and to make music.

Locals and visitors would gather to watch the spectacle of African-Americans dressed in ceremonial garb playing and dancing to traditional music and maintaining a social connection to their home countries and heritages.

The benevolent societies of the 1800s, predecessors to today's insurance companies, were common among many ethnic groups in New Orleans. In exchange for paying dues, a member and his family knew that the society would provide care in times of illness, death, or financial hardship.

The societies also served as charities and community groups, hosting social affairs and providing a sense of unity.

Many of the *Mardi Gras* krewes of today are the descendants of those benevolent societies.

The New Orleans Jazz Funeral is a cultural hybrid arising out of the benevolent societies and the unique role of music in the city's culture.

When one of its members died, a benevolent society would make arrangements for a fitting funeral, which involved hiring a brass band.

On the way to the cemetery, the band would play dirges befitting the somber mood.

In contrast, the march home was more of a parade, with singing and dancing and music to celebrate the life of the member rather than to mourn his death.

The march of people associated with the deceased in a Jazz Funeral, including the family and the band, is referred to as the Main Line.

The Second Line, which augments the celebration, is made up of people who join the parade as part of an organic movement, singing and dancing along the trip back from the cemetery.

**T**oday, a Second Line Parade is one that forms spontaneously, not necessarily part of a funeral, along the streets of New Orleans.

Second Liners frequently carry gaily decorated handkerchiefs, fans, and umbrellas, both as props to use in their dancing and as a first line of defense against the tropical heat of the city.

The Zulu Social Aid and Pleasure Club arose out of the benevolent aid societies of New Orleans.

Originally known as The Tramps, the organization appeared as the Zulus for the first time in 1909.

Louis Armstrong said his lifelong ambition was to be King of the Zulus at a *Mardi Gras* parade, and that wish was fulfilled in 1949.

Before jazz was ragtime.

Before that was Louis Moreau Gottschalk (1829-1869), a New Orleans musician whose syncopated rhythms influenced Scott Joplin and "Jelly Roll" Morton.

Gottschalk, whose father was British and mother was Creole, was exposed to a variety of music at home. He debuted as a performer at age 11.

At 13, he left the United States for classical training in Europe, where Chopin predicted he would be one of the foremost pianists of the century. Gottschalk became the best-known pianist in the New World and the first American musician to be recognized worldwide for his compositions.

He returned to the United States and spent the rest of his life traveling the world, performing and writing music.

**P**rofessor Longhair was the source of sounds that other musicians rode to stardom.

He was born Henry Roeland Byrd in 1918, ahead of his time.

When he played the piano, his music was the earliest inklings of the R&B, funk, and rock-and-roll sounds that did not become popular until the late 1950s.

In 1971, broke and broken, Professor Longhair was sweeping the floor of a record store on Rampart Street when organizers of the New Orleans Jazz and Heritage Festival tracked him down.

He finally began to get the recognition he deserved, enjoying success until his death in 1980.

In 1987, he won a posthumous Grammy, and in 1992 was inducted into the Rock and Roll Hall of Fame.

By the end of World War II, jazz was an established art form, and it was time to start planning a museum to immortalize its origins.

In 1948, some musicians with their own collection of memorabilia formed the New Orleans Jazz Club.

In 1961, when they opened the New Orleans Jazz Museum, the public was eager to see the offerings, and plenty of donors were ready to support it.

In the mid-1970s, when the museum fell on hard financial times, the Louisiana State Museum accepted the entire collection and made it a centerpiece of its exhibitions.

Today, the museum includes instruments of some of the great pioneers, plus photographs, recordings, sheet music, and a collection of jazz posters and paraphernalia.

In the early 1960s, when rock and roll was the rising star, a handful of New Orleans jazz musicians who feared for their art form's survival founded Preservation Hall.

Housed in a building almost as old as the French Quarter itself, Preservation Hall offered a sanctuary where musicians could gather to play and to teach their craft to the next generation.

Opened in 1961, the venue is still popular today, with performances beginning at 8:15 P.M. every day.

To ensure that patrons of Preservation Hall are treated to "one of the last pure music experiences left on the earth," New Orleans jazz is pretty much all that's offered.

The Hall has no air conditioning or bar. No food or drink is available. People who come are there for only one reason: the music.

Many of the charter members of Preservation Hall Jazz Band, the signature ensemble of the Hall, were "second generation" jazz artists who performed with those who invented the art form—Buddy Bolden, "Jelly Roll" Morton, Louis Armstrong, etc.

The PHJB began touring in 1963 and still travels around the world, performing in other classic venues for such honored guests as British royalty, the King of Thailand, and anyone else who recognizes the beauty in what they offer.

New Orleans continues to produce ground-breaking musical talent, and the Neville Brothers are yet another example.

Beginning in the 1950s, the brothers began working in music individually, then together, but lacking any clear direction.

After 20 years of measured success, they came together under the direction of their Uncle George Landry, the Big Chief of The Wild Tchoupitoulas, a *Mardi Gras* Indian tribe.

In 1976, they put together a well-received album based on the call-and-response chants the tribes do on parade. From that event, the Neville Brothers landed a record contract and put out a commercial album the following year.

Today, whether playing solo or making music as a family, the Nevilles have become a New Orleans legend.

ne of the most noted New Orleans nightclubs of the mid-20th century was the Dew Drop Inn at 2836 LaSalle Street. From its opening in 1939 to its demise in 1970, the Dew Drop was a top venue for black performers.

The Dew Drop Inn was actually two buildings, which included a bar room, hotel, restaurant, and barber shop. The structure is still in existence, and it became a local landmark in January 2010.

That same year, the Louisiana Landmarks Society, noting that the Dew Drop was in desperate need of repair and restoration, listed it on its "New Orleans Nine" list of endangered historical treasures.

To commemorate the birth of jazz, artist Robert Dafford was commissioned to paint a series of murals in the 1990s.

Visitors to the Superdome will find one of his works—a 150-foot-tall painting of a clarinet—on the side of a nearby Holiday Inn.

Dedicated May 1, 1996, the giant clarinet is, according to the historic plaque that marks the location, a "modified 'Albert System' model clarinet...similar to those favored by jazz musicians."

The Super Bowl will return to the Superdome in 2013, marking the first time since Hurricane Katrina that the NFL Championship game will be held in New Orleans.

This will be the seventh time the game has been held in the Superdome. The dates of the other Superdome Super Bowls are 1978, 1981, 1986, 1990, 1997, and 2002.

During Hurricane Katrina, the Louisiana Superdome was considered the "refuge of last resort." It was a designation that had been used before to describe the behemoth, but nothing had ever tested it the way the storm would.

As many as 30,000 people were huddled in the Superdome during the week it was used as a lifeboat in the flooded city. Some refugees were there for seven days as the electricity failed, the water and food supplies dwindled, the sanitation facilities overflowed, and the mood got ugly.

When it was all over, reports of murders, rapes, and riots turned out to have been greatly exaggerated. The survivors from the Superdome had endured hellish conditions, but the feared anarchy never really materialized.

While 30,000 people were known to be waiting for rescue in the Superdome, another 19,000 people had gathered for shelter at the New Orleans Convention Center.

No food, water, medical supplies, or security personnel had been stationed at the Convention Center, and rescuers did not know anyone was there.

The Convention Center was evacuated one week after Katrina hit New Orleans.

For some, the reconstruction of the Superdome after Hurricane Katrina was a waste of resources. For others, it represented the resilience of the people of New Orleans.

By September 2006, barely a year after the storm had ripped the stadium apart, the Superdome was ready to host the New Orleans Saints' season opener.

By the start of the 2010 season, the Superdome was being called one of the most fan-friendly stadiums in the country, and many national sporting events—from NCAA basketball to the 2013 Super Bowl—were being scheduled there.

**T**he National Football League admitted the New Orleans team to the league in 1966 on All Saints Day (November 1).

The owners of the team felt it only fitting that the team name should reflect the "day it was born," and the team was christened the New Orleans Saints.

In their first game, on September 17, 1967, the Saints returned the opening kickoff for a 94-yard touchdown.

Things definitely went downhill after that, though, and the Saints ended their first season with a 3-11 record.

In their first year in the Superdome (1975), the team did even worse, with a 2-12 record.

But all of that really doesn't matter anymore, since the New Orleans Saints won the 2010 Super Bowl.

**193**

NEW ORLEANS
FACTS

ew Orleans: the home of Jazz, *Mardi Gras*, and...dental floss.

Yes, it was way back in 1819 when New Orleans dentist Levi Spear Parmly said that running waxed silk thread between the teeth was probably the single most effective way of preventing tooth decay.

Dr. Parmly didn't file for a patent on his invention or market it to the public; that didn't happen for another couple of generations.

But when it comes to saying "I told you so" with a healthy smile, Dr. Parmly gets to be leader of the pack.

In 1884, the latest thing in dentistry was a new-fangled motorized drill with a flexible shaft. It was attached to the chair and had a foot pedal so the dentist could turn it on and off without taking his hands out of his patient's mouth.

That was all Dr. C. Edmund Kells in New Orleans needed to know. He could see the future, and he made it happen.

Striking a deal with the local streetcar company, the thoroughly modern Dr. Kells tapped into its electricity to build the first all-electric dentist office.

In the early 1800s, anyone could open up a pharmacy and begin selling tonics and ointments "for whatever ails ya." There were no standards or regulations.

So when Louisiana established a licensing examination for pharmacists and Louis Dufilho Jr. passed it in 1823, he became the first licensed pharmacist in the country.

His shop became the Pharmacy Museum in 1950, and today it contains the nation's largest pharmaceutical collection.

The word *lagniappe* (pronounced *lan-yap*) is common in New Orleans.

It refers to a little something extra thrown into a bargain at no additional cost, a customary practice among merchants—similar to the 13th item in a baker's dozen.

Mark Twain found the word "worth traveling to New Orleans to get," explaining the term in his 1883 *Life on the Mississippi*.

For *lagniappe*:

The oldest continuously running

community theatre in the country is

on Jackson Square in the French Quarter.

Shows have been appearing at

Le Petit Theatre since 1916.

## ABOUT THE AUTHOR

Victor Dorff is a New Yorker living in Southern California and writing about the travel destinations that make the world such an interesting place to visit. His work has been seen on television, on the web, and on bookshelves around the country. He can be seen in airports, hotels, museums, restaurants, or any-where a good story being told.